W9-AUW-805

# RICHARD SCARRY'S

# BUSY KIDS
# Explore Reading, Writing, and Phonics!

Featuring new illustrations
by Huck Scarry

RiverStream

RiverStream Publishing and the distinctive RiverStream Publishing logo
are registered trademarks of RiverStream Publishing, Inc.

Copyright © 2013 Richard Scarry Corporation, all illustrations.
Copyright © 2013 Dancing Penguins, LLC, all text.

All characters are property of Richard Scarry Corporation.

All rights reserved. No part of this publication may be reproduced, stored in a retrieval system, or
transmitted, in any form or by any means, electronic, mechanical, photocopying, recording, or
otherwise, without prior written permission from the publisher. Purchase of this book for
classroom use allows pages to be reproduced for classroom use only.

ISBN 978-1-62243-093-2

Published in 2013 by RiverStream Publishing Company, Inc.
By arrangement with Dancing Penguins, LLC
On behalf of the Richard Scarry Corporation

Library of Congress Cataloging-in-Publication Data on file with the Publisher.

 a Dancing Penguins • J R Sansevere Book

Written by Erica Farber
Designed by Matthew Rossetti
Covers designed by Gina Fujita

1 2 3 4 5 GPP 16 15 14 13

RiverStream Publishing—Globus Printing & Packaging
Minster, OH—052013—1010GPPSP13

www.riverstreampublishing.net

# Meet the Busy Kids of Busytown!

Froggy

Lowly

Bridget

Huckle

Arthur

Ella

Molly

Frances

Skip

Goldbug

Miss Honey

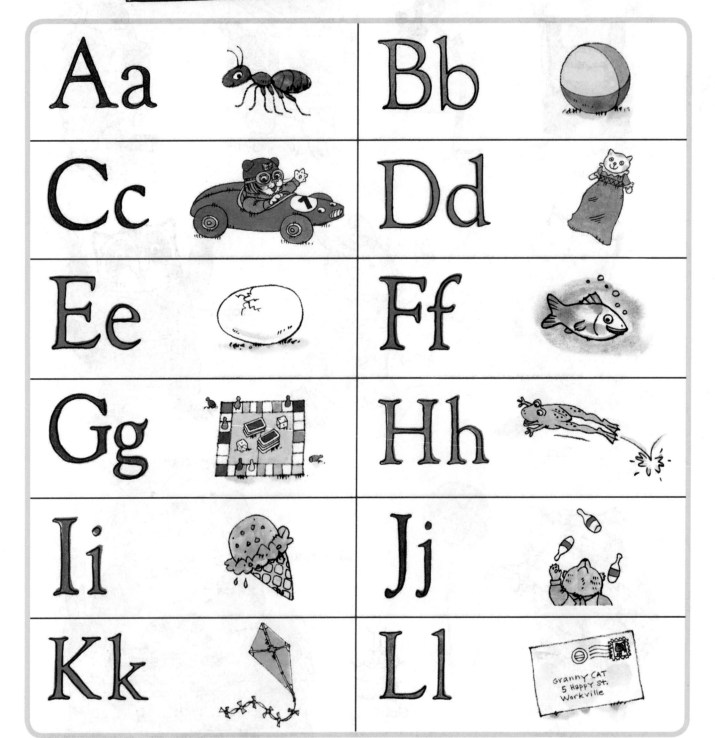

| | |
|---|---|
| Aa | Bb |
| Cc | Dd |
| Ee | Ff |
| Gg | Hh |
| Ii | Jj |
| Kk | Ll |

Granny CAT
5 HappY St.
Workville

| Mm | | Nn | 12345 67890 |
|---|---|---|---|
| Oo | | Pp | PINK |
| Qq | | Rr | |
| Ss | | Tt | |
| Uu | | Vv | |
| Ww | | Xx | |
| Yy | | Zz | |

## My Name

Huckle and his friends are at the Busytown Library. Huckle is reading a book all about busy, colorful trains. Can you help him practice his letter sounds for **A, B,** and **C**?

Draw a line from each letter to the picture that begins with the same letter.

# Aa

# Bb

# Cc

**A**wesome! Trace the letters Aa, Bb, and Cc.

How many letters are in the alphabet?

11.
T-H-E-A-L-P-H-A-B-E-T

Aa Bb Cc

# Aa

Aa Aa Aa Aa Aa

# Bb

Bb Bb Bb Bb Bb

# Cc

Cc Cc Cc Cc Cc

Then write the letters yourself. Bravo!

## My Name

Arthur is reading a book about trains, too! It is **d**aring, **e**xciting, and **f**un! Can you help him practice his letter sounds for **D, E,** and **F**?

Draw a line from each letter to the picture that begins with the same letter.

# Dd

# Ee

# Ff

## My Name

**E**xcellent! Now, trace the letters Dd, Ee, and Ff.

# Dd

Dd Dd Dd Dd Dd

# Ee

Ee Ee Ee Ee Ee Ee

# Ff

Ff Ff Ff Ff Ff Ff

Then write the letters yourself. Fantastic!

## My Name

Molly is reading a book about a **green**, **h**ungry, **i**cky dragon. She needs to practice her letter sounds for **G, H,** and **I**. Can you help her?

Draw a line from each letter to the picture that begins with the same letter.

# Gg

# Hh

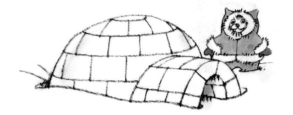

# Ii

## My Name

Great! Now, trace the letters Gg, Hh, and Ii.

# Gg

Gg Gg Gg Gg Gg

# Hh

Hh Hh Hh Hh Hh

# Ii

Ii Ii Ii Ii Ii Ii Ii

Then write the letters yourself. Hooray!

## My Name

Skip is not reading. He is bouncing a ball. Shh, Skip! Do not juggle or kick that ball. It is too loud for the library! Can you help Skip practice the sounds for **J, K,** and **L**?

Draw a line from each letter to the picture that begins with the same letter.

Jj

Kk

Ll

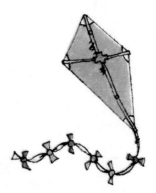

## My Name

Good job! Now, trace the letters Jj, Kk, and Ll.

**Jj**

Jj Jj Jj Jj Jj Jj Jj

**Kk**

Kk Kk Kk Kk Kk Kk Kk

**Ll**

Ll Ll Ll Ll Ll Ll Ll

Then write the letters yourself. Lovely!

## My Name

Bridget is checking out a **m**ystery book that is **n**ot too long **o**r too short. Can you help her review the letter sounds for **M, N,** and **O**?

Draw a line from each letter to the picture that begins with the same letter.

Marvelous! Now, trace the letters Mm, Nn, and Oo.

# Mm

Mm Mm Mm Mm

# Nn

Nn Nn Nn Nn Nn

# Oo

Oo Oo Oo Oo Oo

Then write the letters yourself. Nice!

## My Name

Ella is telling her doll a story. It is about a prince, a queen, and a ring. She is working on the letter sounds for **P, Q,** and **R**. Can you help her?

Draw a line from each letter to the picture that begins with the same letter.

# Pp

# Qq

# Rr

**R**eally **q**uite **p**erfect! Now, trace the letters Pp, Qq, and Rr.

Pp

Pp  Pp  Pp  Pp  Pp

Qq

Qq  Qq  Qq  Qq  Qq

Rr

Rr  Rr  Rr  Rr  Rr

Then write the letters yourself. Perfect!

## My Name

Lowly is reading a joke book. His favorite joke is: Where do books **sleep**? **T**hey sleep **u**nder their covers! **S**illy Lowly! He is practicing his **S, T,** and **U** sounds.

Draw a line from each letter to the picture that begins with the same letter.

 Ss

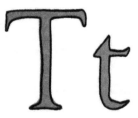 Tt

 Uu

## My Name

Terrific! Now trace the letters Ss, Tt, and Uu.

# Ss

Ss Ss Ss Ss Ss Ss

# Tt

Tt Tt Tt Tt Tt Tt

# Uu

Uu Uu Uu Uu Uu Uu

Then write the letters yourself. Splendid!

## My Name

Careful, Frances! Miss Honey is worried your **v**olcano **w**ill e**x**plode. Can you help Frances practice the letter sounds for **V, W,** and **X**?

Draw a line from each letter to the picture that begins with the same letter.

## My Name

Wow! Now trace the letters Vv, Ww, and Xx.

# Vv

# Ww

# Xx

Then write the letters yourself. Wonderful!

## My Name

Lowly really likes the letters **Y** and **Z**! **Y**es, he does. See him **z**igzag. Help him practice the letter sounds for **Y** and **Z**.

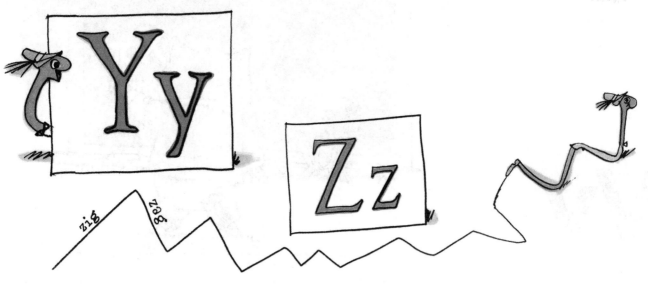

zig zag

Draw a line from each letter to the picture that begins with the same letter.

## My Name

Yay for you! Now trace the letters Yy and Zz.

# Yy

Yy  Yy  Yy  Yy  Yy  Yy

# Zz

Zz  Zz  Zz  Zz  Zz  Zz

Then write the letters yourself. Yes!

# Long and Short Vowels

Help Molly learn her long and short vowels—right after she catches her bike! Is the **a** in catch long or short? If you said short, you would be right! Is the **i** in bike long or short? If you said long, you would be right again!

Now look at the pictures on these two pages. Color the pictures with short vowels **red**. Color the pictures with long vowels **blue**.

# Long and Short Vowels

## My Name

# Stuck in the Middle: Short Vowels

Oh, no! There goes Lowly's hat! **Hat** has a short **a** as a middle sound. Can you circle the pictures below that have a short **a** as a middle sound?

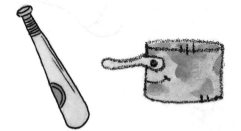   

Huckle has a hen on his head. Silly hen! **Hen** has a short **e** as a middle sound. Can you circle the pictures below that have a short **e** as a middle sound?

26

# Stuck in the Middle: Short Vowels

See Molly sit in her carrot car. **Sit** has a short i as a middle sound. Can you circle the pictures below that have a short i as a middle sound?

See Bridget's tire pop! **Pop** has a short o as a middle sound. Can you circle the pictures below that have a short o as a middle sound?

Ella likes to hug her doll. **Hug** has a short u as a middle sound. Can you circle the pictures below that have a short u as a middle sound?

# Stuck in the Middle: Long Vowels

See Arthur skateboard. **Skate** has a long **a** as a middle sound. Can you circle the pictures in the box below that have a long **a** as a middle sound?

Huckle and his friends go to Cheese Street. **Cheese** and **Street** both have a long **e** as their middle sound. Can you circle the pictures below that have a long **e** as a middle sound?

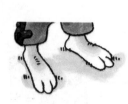    

# Stuck in the Middle: Long Vowels

 Arthur, stop reading and keep your eyes on that bike! You remember that **bike** has a long i as a middle sound, right? Circle the pictures below that have a long i as their middle sound.

 Careful, Mr. Pig! Don't drive that boat too fast! **Boat** has a long o as a middle sound. Circle the pictures below that have a long o as their middle sound.

 Doesn't Lowly look cute when he is sleeping? **Cute** has a long u as a middle sound. Circle the pictures below that have a long u as their middle sound.

# Find the Ending Sounds

Huckle and Lowly are practicing their ending sounds. Can you help them?

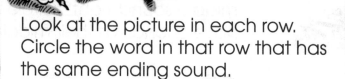

Look at the picture in each row.
Circle the word in that row that has
the same ending sound.

| | | | | |
|---|---|---|---|---|
| | fan | hat | log | goat |
| | hat | fog | bug | top |
| | shell | sun | brain | pan |
| | box | map | top | hat |
| | pan | goat | bat | map |

## My Name

Look! There is a letter in Huckle's book. **Look** and **book** have the same ending sound.

Look at the picture in the first row. Say the name of the picture. Then look for the picture in the second row that has the same ending sound as the one in the first row. Draw a line from the picture in the first row to the picture in the second row that has the same ending sound.

## My Name

Huckle and Lowly show Miss Elephant a letter. What is the ending sound of the word **letter**? If you said **r** you would be right. Help Huckle and Lowly review their ending sounds.

Say the name of each picture. Listen to its ending sound. Write the letter to complete each word. Then say the word out loud.

| | |
|---|---|
| be _ _ _ _ | han _ _ _ _ |
| bu _ _ _ _ | lo _ _ _ _ |
| su _ _ _ _ | yar _ _ _ _ |
| goa _ _ _ _ | nes _ _ _ _ |

## My Name

Huckle and his friends look at a letter. **Letter** begins with the **l** sound and ends with the **r** sound, as you already know.

Draw a line from each picture to its beginning and ending sounds.

t____n

h____t

n____t

b____g

m____p

g____t

## My Name

Oops! Skip falls and off falls his hat. **Hat** has **h** as a beginning sound and **t** as an ending sound.

Say the name of each picture. Then write the letter of its beginning and ending sounds.

\_\_\_\_\_ **a** \_\_\_\_\_

\_\_\_\_\_ **u** \_\_\_\_\_

\_\_\_\_\_ **an** \_\_\_\_\_

\_\_\_\_\_ **e** \_\_\_\_\_

\_\_\_\_\_ **o** \_\_\_\_\_

\_\_\_\_\_ **o** \_\_\_\_\_

# Word Families: –at

Huckle Cat is part of the Cat family. His last name **Cat** ends in **at,** which makes it part of the **–at** word family.

Use the letters in the box below to help Huckle Cat build new words in the **–at** word family.

> m     f     b     h

_____
___ at

_____
___ at

_____
___ at

_____
___ at

# Word Families: –it

Huckle **fit** a big pumpkin in a small wagon. **Fit** ends in **–it** which means **fit** belongs in the **–it** word family. Can you name more words that end in **–it**?

Use the letters in the box below to build new words that end in **–it**.

> s     k     l     h

___

\_\_\_\_\_ **it**          \_\_\_\_\_ **it**


\_\_\_\_\_ **it**          \_\_\_\_\_ **it**

# Word Families: –op

Officer Flossy holds up her stop sign. She wants Molly's bike to stop rolling away. Stop! **Stop** ends in **–op** which means it is part of the **–op** word family. Can you name more words that end in **–op**?

Use the letters in the box below to build new words that end in **–op**.

| m | t | p | h |
|---|---|---|---|

_____ **op**          _____ **op**

_____ **op**          _____ **op**

# Word Families: –ug

Goldbug is one busy bug! **Bug** ends in **–ug**, which means it is part of the **–ug** word family. Can you help Goldbug write more words that end in **–ug**?

Use the letters in the box below to build new words that end in **–ug**.

j     r     m     h

_____ **ug**          _____ **ug**

_____ **ug**          _____ **ug**

# Word Families: –ill

Huckle and Lowly are **still** asleep. When **will** they wake up? **Will** and **still** end in **–ill**, which means they are part of the **–ill** word family.

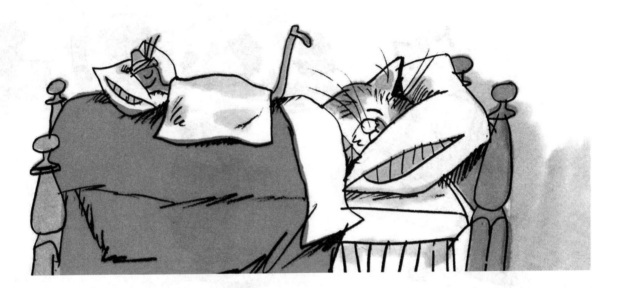

Use the letters in the box below to build new words that end in **–ill**.

| h | f | ch | dr |

_____ **ill**          _____ **ill**

_____ **ill**          _____ **ill**

**My Name**

# Word Families: –ar

Oh, no! How will Huckle, Lowly, and Bridget catch up with the garbage truck? It is **far, far** away! **Far** ends in **–ar**, which means it is part of the **–ar** word family.

Can you build new words that end in **–ar** using the letters in the box?

> j      c      b      st

_____ ar       _____ ar

_____ ar       _____ ar

# Sequencing: Order of Events

Huckle and Bridget are baking a cake for Lowly's birthday. How will the cake turn out? Put a **1** under the picture that shows what happens **first**. Put a **2** under the picture that shows what happens **second**. Put a **3** under what happens **third**, and put a **4** under the picture that shows what happens **last**.

## My Name

Fill in the sentences below to find out what happens when Huckle goes to the library. Use the word bank to help you.

**Word Bank**

letter    bike    garden    book

Huckle is reading a _____ .

Skip is riding a _____ .

Crash! Huckle and Skip fall.
A _____ falls out of the book.

Huckle takes the letter to Miss Mouse who is in her _____ .

## My Name

Fill in the sentences below to find out what happens after Miss Mouse reads the letter. Use the word bank to help you.

**Word Bank**

talks    cone    cream    train

Miss Mouse, Huckle, and his friends go to see Toot. Toot fixes the _____.

Toot _____ to Miss Mouse.

Toot and Miss Mouse eat ice _____.

Huckle has a chocolate _____.

# Sequencing: Order of Events

How did that letter get in Huckle's library book? It's a mystery. Put a **1** under the picture that shows what happens **first**. Put a **2** under the picture that shows what happens **second**. Put a **3** under what happens **third**, and put a **4** under the picture that shows what happens **last**.

## My Name

Oh, no! Miss Mouse mixed up the seeds for her garden. Can you help her?

Draw a line to match the name of each vegetable to the right pack of seeds.

Lettuce

Carrots

Peppers

Peas

## My Name _____

It's Saturday. Hooray! Fill in the blanks to find out about Huckle's fun day. Use the word bank to help you.

**Word Bank**

story     play     sleep     lunch

Huckle and Lowly _____ ball.

At twelve o'clock, they eat _____ .

Father Cat reads a bedtime _____ .

Huckle and Lowly go to _____ .

## My Name

Arthur, Huckle, Bridget, and Lowly eat ice cream at the ice cream shop. Write the kind of ice cream each one is eating. Use the word bank to help you.

**Word Bank**

chocolate      berry      mint      vanilla

_____

_____

_____

_____

## My Name

Here is Toot's letter to Miss Mouse. And here is Goldbug to teach you how to write a **friendly letter**. In Toot's letter, he invites Miss Mouse to have ice cream.

Toot forgot the DATE. How about April Fools! Hee! Hee!

April 1, 2013

The GREETING

Dear Miss Mouse,

The BODY

Do you want to get some ice cream?

The CLOSING

YOUR NAME or your SIGNATURE if you like to write cursive!

From,
Toot

# Write a Friendly Letter

Now, you write a letter to one of your friends. In your letter, invite your friend to have ice cream. Don't forget to put the date at the top!

Dear                    ,

From,

## My Name

Huckle and Lowly look at the letter Toot wrote to Miss Mouse. Miss Mouse's address is on the front. Huckle and Lowly want to send a letter to Molly Bunny. Can you help them address the letter? Use the words in the word bank to help you.

**Word Bank**

Molly   Street

Carrot   Busytown

# Write a Thank You

Miss Mouse needs to write a thank you note to Toot. She wants to thank him for taking her for ice cream. She also wants to tell him it was fun. Can you help her write it? The thank you note has been started for you.

Dear Toot,

Thank you for

                                    .

It was              .

            From,

Huckle and his friends are at the Busytown Library. Huckle is reading a book all about busy, colorful trains. Can you help him practice his letter sounds for **A, B,** and **C**?

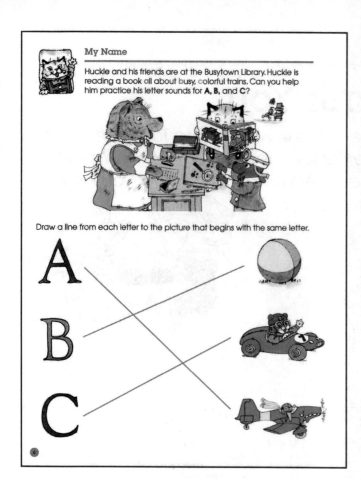

Draw a line from each letter to the picture that begins with the same letter.

A
B
C

---

Trace the letters Aa, Bb, and Cc.

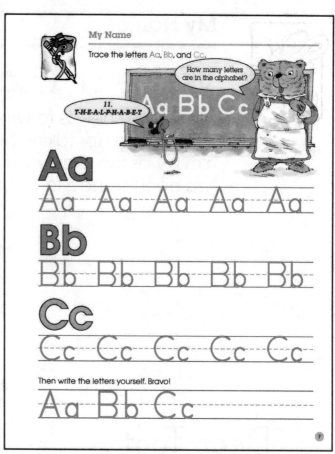

How many letters are in the alphabet?

11. T-H-E-A-L-P-H-A-B-E-T

Aa Bb Cc

**Aa**
Aa Aa Aa Aa Aa

**Bb**
Bb Bb Bb Bb Bb

**Cc**
Cc Cc Cc Cc Cc

Then write the letters yourself. Bravo!

Aa Bb Cc

---

Arthur is reading a book about trains, too! It is daring, exciting, and fun! Can you help him practice his letter sounds for **D, E,** and **F**?

Draw a line from each letter to the picture that begins with the same letter.

D
E
F

---

Excellent! Now, trace the letters Dd, Ee, and Ff.

**Dd**
Dd Dd Dd Dd Dd

**Ee**
Ee Ee Ee Ee Ee Ee

**Ff**
Ff Ff Ff Ff Ff Ff

Then write the letters yourself. Fantastic!

Dd Ee Ff

Molly is reading a book about a green, hungry, icky dragon. She needs to practice her letter sounds for **G, H,** and **I.** Can you help her?

Draw a line from each letter to the picture that begins with the same letter.

G

H

I

Great! Now, trace the letters Gg, Hh, and Ii.

**Gg**

Gg Gg Gg Gg Gg

**Hh**

Hh Hh Hh Hh Hh

**Ii**

Ii Ii Ii Ii Ii Ii

Then write the letters yourself. Hooray!

Gg Hh Ii

Skip is not reading. He is bouncing a ball. Shh, Skip! Do not juggle or kick that ball. It is too loud for the library! Can you help Skip practice the sounds for **J, K,** and **L?**

Draw a line from each letter to the picture that begins with the same letter.

Jj

Kk

Ll

Good job! Now, trace the letters Jj, Kk, and Ll.

**Jj**

Jj Jj Jj Jj Jj Jj

**Kk**

Kk Kk Kk Kk Kk Kk

**Ll**

Then write the letters yourself. Lovely!

Jj Kk Ll

Bridget is checking out a mystery book that is not too long or too short. Can you help her review the letter sounds for **M**, **N**, and **O**?

Draw a line from each letter to the picture that begins with the same letter.

Mm

Nn

Oo

Marvelous! Now, trace the letters Mm, Nn, and Oo.

**Mm**

Mm Mm Mm Mm

**Nn**

Nn Nn Nn Nn Nn

**Oo**

Oo Oo Oo Oo Oo

Then write the letters yourself. Nice!

Mm Nn Oo

Ella is telling her doll a story. It is about a prince, a queen, and a ring. She is working on the letter sounds for **P**, **Q**, and **R**. Can you help her?

Draw a line from each letter to the picture that begins with the same letter.

Pp

Qq

Rr

Really quite perfect! Now, trace the letters Pp, Qq, and Rr.

**Pp**

Pp Pp Pp Pp Pp

**Qq**

Qq Qq Qq Qq Qq

**Rr**

Rr Rr Rr Rr Rr

Then write the letters yourself. Perfect!

Pp Qq Rr

**My Name** _____

Lowly is reading a joke book. His favorite joke is: Where do books sleep? They sleep under their covers! Silly Lowly! He is practicing his **S, T,** and **U** sounds.

Draw a line from each letter to the picture that begins with the same letter.

S s

T t

U u

**My Name** _____

Terrific! Now trace the letters Ss, Tt, and Uu.

Then write the letters yourself. Splendid!

**My Name** _____

Careful, Frances! Miss Honey is worried your volcano will explode. Can you help Frances practice the letter sounds for **V, W,** and **X**?

Draw a line from each letter to the picture that begins with the same letter.

V v

W w

X x

**My Name** _____

Wow! Now trace the letters Vv, Ww, and Xx.

Then write the letters yourself. Wonderful!

Lowly really likes the letters **Y** and **Z**! Yes, he does. See him zigzag. Help him practice the letter sounds for **Y** and **Z**.

Draw a line from each letter to the picture that begins with the same letter.

Yay for you! Now trace the letters Yy and Zz.

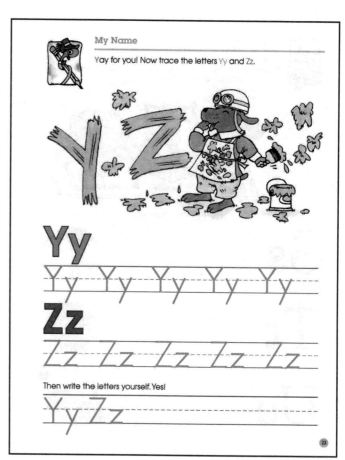

Yy

Y y  Y y  Y y  Y y  Y y

Zz

Z z  Z z  Z z  Z z  Z z

Then write the letters yourself. Yes!

Y y Z z

# Long and Short Vowels

Help Molly learn her long and short vowels—right after she catches her bike! Is the a in catch long or short? If you said short, you would be right! Is the i in bike long or short? If you said long, you would be right again!

Now look at the pictures on these two pages. Color the pictures with short vowels red. Color the pictures with long vowels blue.

red

red

blue

blue

# Long and Short Vowels

blue

blue

red

red

blue

blue

blue

red

# Stuck in the Middle: Short Vowels

Oh, no! There goes Lowly's hat! **Hat** has a short a as a middle sound. Can you circle the pictures below that have a short a as a middle sound?

Huckle has a hen on his head. Silly hen! **Hen** has a short e as a middle sound. Can you circle the pictures below that have a short e as a middle sound?

---

# Stuck in the Middle: Short Vowels

See Molly sit in her carrot car. **Sit** has a short i as a middle sound. Can you circle the pictures below that have a short i as a middle sound?

See Bridget's tire pop! **Pop** has a short o as a middle sound. Can you circle the pictures below that have a short o as a middle sound?

Ella likes to hug her doll. **Hug** has a short u as a middle sound. Can you circle the pictures below that have a short u as a middle sound?

---

# Stuck in the Middle: Long Vowels

See Arthur skateboard. **Skate** has a long a as a middle sound. Can you circle the pictures in the box below that have a long a as a middle sound?

Huckle and his friends go to Cheese Street. **Cheese** and **Street** both have a long e as their middle sound. Can you circle the pictures below that have a long e as a middle sound?

---

# Stuck in the Middle: Long Vowels

Arthur, stop reading and keep your eyes on that bike! You remember that **bike** has a long i as a middle sound, right? Circle the pictures below that have a long i as their middle sound.

Careful, Mr. Pig! Don't drive that boat too fast! **Boat** has a long o as a middle sound. Circle the pictures below that have a long o as their middle sound.

Doesn't Lowly look cute when he is sleeping? **Cute** has a long u as a middle sound. Circle the pictures below that have a long u as their middle sound.

# Find the Ending Sounds

Huckle and Lowly are practicing their ending sounds. Can you help them?

Look at the picture in each row. Circle the word in that row that has the same ending sound.

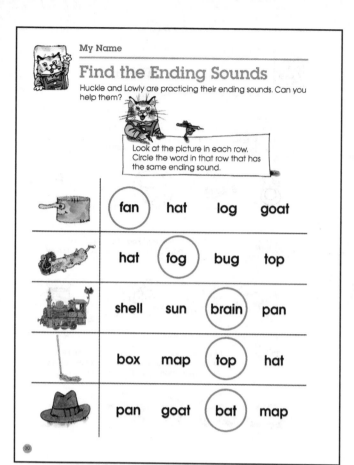

| | | | | |
|---|---|---|---|---|
| | (fan) | hat | log | goat |
| | hat | (fog) | bug | top |
| | shell | sun | (brain) | pan |
| | box | map | (top) | hat |
| | pan | goat | (bat) | map |

---

Look! There is a letter in Huckle's book. **Look** and **book** have the same ending sound.

Look at the picture in the first row. Say the name of the picture. Then look for the picture in the second row that has the same ending sound as the one in the first row. Draw a line from the picture in the first row to the picture in the second row that has the same ending sound.

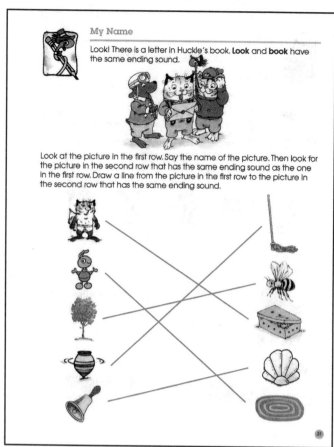

---

Huckle and Lowly show Miss Elephant a letter. What is the ending sound of the word **letter**? If you said **r** you would be right. Help Huckle and Lowly review their ending sounds.

Say the name of each picture. Listen to its ending sound. Write the letter to complete each word. Then say the word out loud.

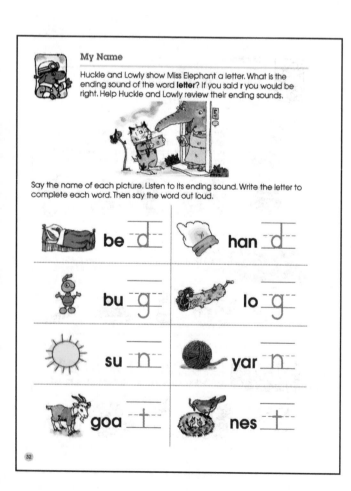

| | | | |
|---|---|---|---|
| be d | han d |
| bu g | lo g |
| su n | yar n |
| goa t | nes t |

---

Huckle and his friends look at a letter. **Letter** begins with the **l** sound and ends with the **r** sound, as you already know.

Draw a line from each picture to its beginning and ending sounds.

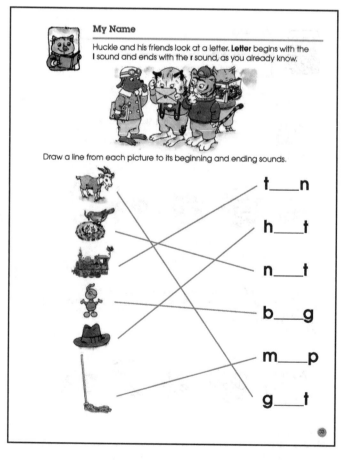

t___n

h___t

n___t

b___g

m___p

g___t

Oops! Skip falls and off falls his hat. **Hat** has **h** as a beginning sound and **t** as an ending sound.

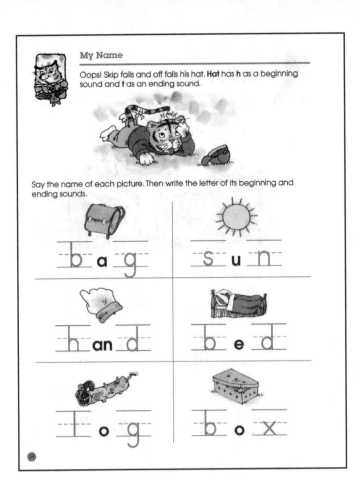

Say the name of each picture. Then write the letter of its beginning and ending sounds.

**b** a **g**       **s** u **n**

**h** an **d**       **b** e **d**

**f** o **g**       **b** o **x**

---

# Word Families: –at

Huckle Cat is part of the Cat family. His last name **Cat** ends in **at**, which makes it part of the **-at** word family.

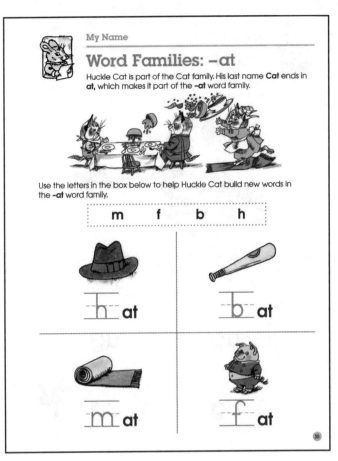

Use the letters in the box below to help Huckle Cat build new words in the **-at** word family.

m     f     b     h

**h** at       **b** at

**m** at       **f** at

---

# Word Families: –it

Huckle **fit** a big pumpkin in a small wagon. **Fit** ends in **-it** which means **fit** belongs in the **-it** word family. Can you name more words that end in **-it**?

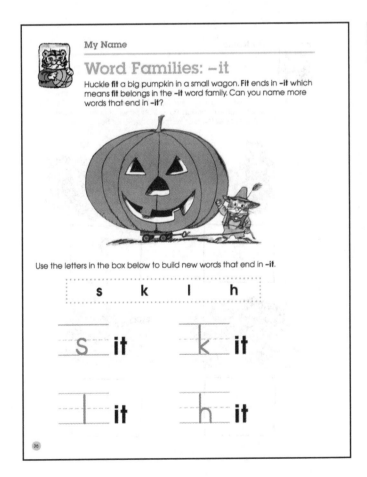

Use the letters in the box below to build new words that end in **-it**.

s     k     l     h

**s** it       **k** it

**l** it       **h** it

---

# Word Families: –op

Officer Flossy holds up her stop sign. She wants Molly's bike to stop rolling away. Stop! **Stop** ends in **-op** which means it is part of the **-op** word family. Can you name more words that end in **-op**?

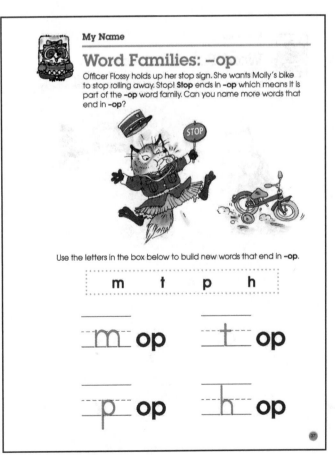

Use the letters in the box below to build new words that end in **-op**.

m     t     p     h

**m** op       **t** op

**p** op       **h** op

# Word Families: –ug

Goldbug is one busy bug! **Bug** ends in **–ug**, which means it is part of the **–ug** word family. Can you help Goldbug write more words that end in **–ug**?

Use the letters in the box below to build new words that end in **–ug**.

```
j    r    m    h
```

j ug          r ug

m ug          h ug

# Word Families: –ill

Huckle and Lowly are **still** asleep. When **will** they wake up? **Will** and **still** end in **–ill**, which means they are part of the **–ill** word family.

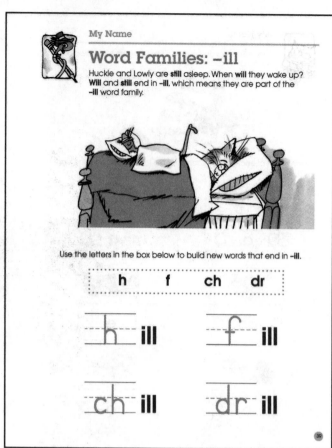

Use the letters in the box below to build new words that end in **–ill**.

```
h    f    ch    dr
```

h ill          f ill

ch ill          dr ill

# Word Families: –ar

Oh, no! How will Huckle, Lowly, and Bridget catch up with the garbage truck? It is **far, far** away! **Far** ends in **–ar**, which means it is part of the **–ar** word family.

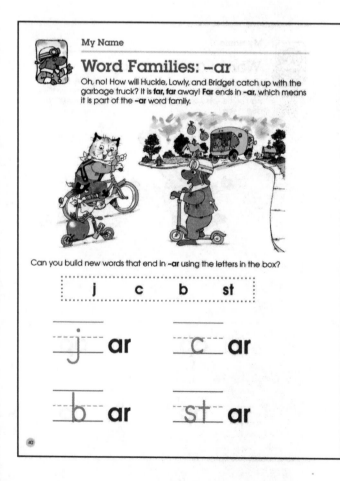

Can you build new words that end in **–ar** using the letters in the box?

```
j    c    b    st
```

j ar          c ar

b ar          st ar

# Sequencing: Order of Events

Huckle and Bridget are baking a cake for Lowly's birthday. How will the cake turn out? Put a **1** under the picture that shows what happens **first**. Put a **2** under the picture that shows what happens **second**. Put a **3** under what happens **third**, and put a **4** under the picture that shows what happens **last**.

2          3

4          1

Fill in the sentences below to find out what happens when Huckle goes to the library. Use the word bank to help you.

**Word Bank**
letter    bike    garden    book

Huckle is reading a ___book___ .

Skip is riding a ___bike___ .

Crash! Huckle and Skip fall. A ___letter___ falls out of the book.

Huckle takes the letter to Miss Mouse who is in her ___garden___ .

---

Fill in the sentences below to find out what happens after Miss Mouse reads the letter. Use the word bank to help you.

**Word Bank**
talks    cone    cream    train

Miss Mouse, Huckle, and his friends go to see Toot. Toot fixes the ___train___ .

Toot ___talks___ to Miss Mouse.

Toot and Miss Mouse eat ice ___cream___ .

Huckle has a chocolate ___cone___ .

---

## Sequencing: Order of Events

How did that letter get in Huckle's library book? It's a mystery. Put a **1** under the picture that shows what happens **first**. Put a **2** under the picture that shows what happens **second**. Put a **3** under what happens **third**, and put a **4** under the picture that shows what happens **last**.

3    1

4    2

---

Oh, no! Miss Mouse mixed up the seeds for her garden. Can you help her?

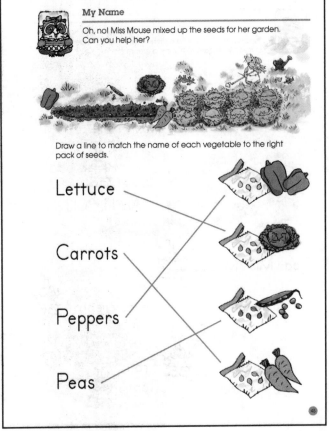

Draw a line to match the name of each vegetable to the right pack of seeds.

Lettuce

Carrots

Peppers

Peas

It's Saturday. Hooray! Fill in the blanks to find out about Huckle's fun day. Use the word bank to help you.

**Word Bank**

story    play    sleep    lunch

Huckle and Lowly ___play___ ball.

At twelve o'clock, they eat ___lunch___.

Father Cat reads a bedtime ___story___.

Huckle and Lowly go to ___sleep___.

46

---

Arthur, Huckle, Bridget, and Lowly eat ice cream at the ice cream shop. Write the kind of ice cream each one is eating. Use the word bank to help you.

**Word Bank**

chocolate    berry    mint    vanilla

| berry | vanilla |
| mint | chocolate |

47

---

Here is Toot's letter to Miss Mouse. And here is Goldbug to teach you how to write a **friendly letter**. In Toot's letter, he invites Miss Mouse to have ice cream.

Dear Miss Mouse,

Do you want to get some ice cream?

April 1, 2013

The GREETING

The BODY

Toot forgot the DATE. How about April Fools! Hee! Hee!

The CLOSING

YOUR NAME or your SIGNATURE if you like to write cursive!

From,
Toot

48

---

# Write a Friendly Letter

Now, you write a letter to one of your friends. In your letter, invite your friend to have ice cream. Don't forget to put the date at the top!

date

Dear _____ ,

answers will vary

From,

name

49

---